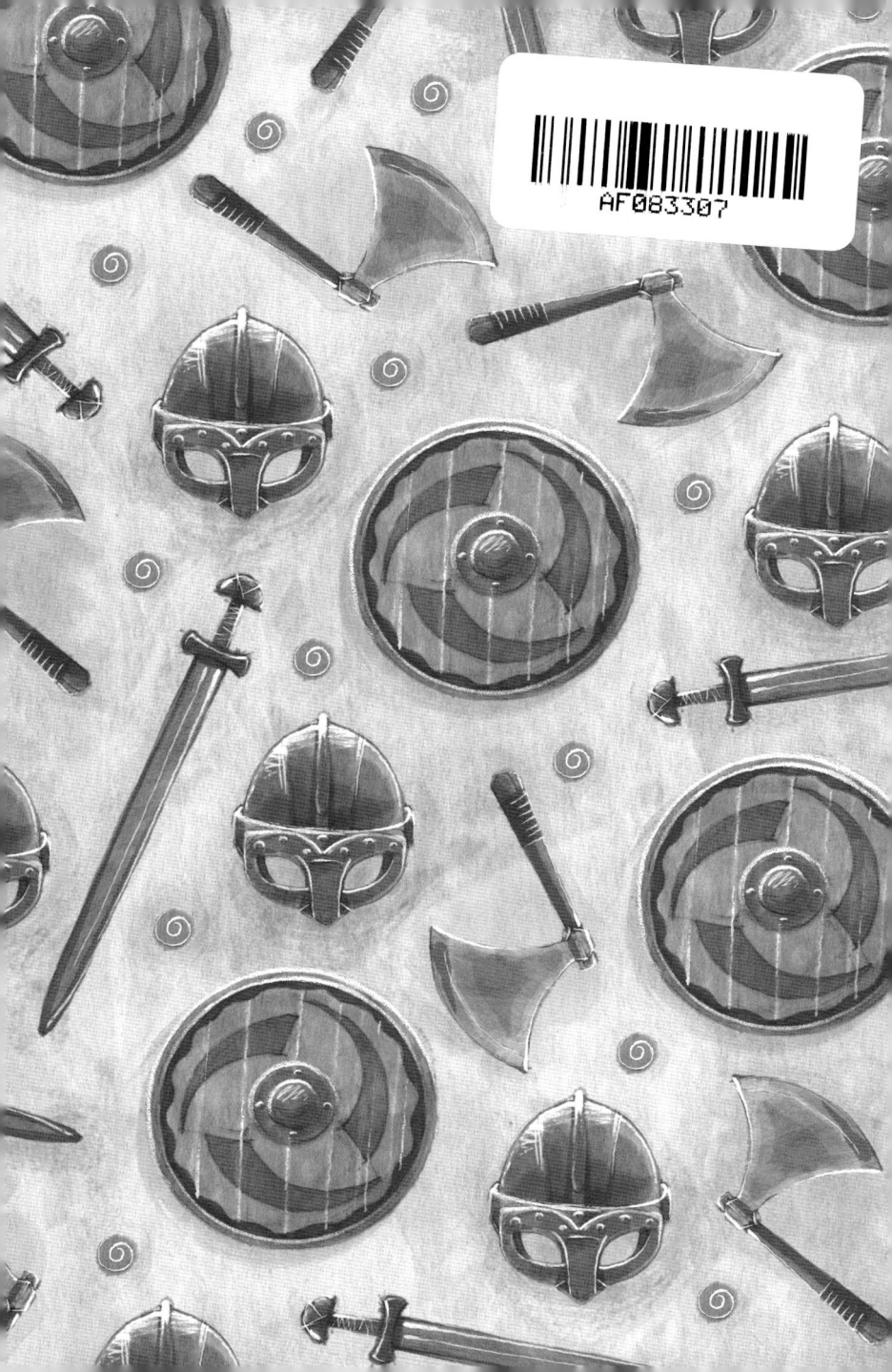

SEA WOLF

Chris Bradford
Illustrated by Eugenia Nobati

Collins

1. Wolf pup

The sky was growing dark above the ice-crusted hills of Greenland. Sven stood alone and shivering, a crooked stick in one hand. He watched over the sheep huddled together on the rocky slope as a chill breeze blew off the ocean. The air smelt of sea salt and sheep dung. He stamped his feet to stay warm, his sealskin **turnshoes** too thin to keep out the cold.

A long, low howl echoed from the darkening hills. Sven froze. Not from cold, but fear. Another howl followed. Closer this time. His eyes wide, Sven peered into the shadows beneath a patch of juniper bushes nearby. The sheep bleated nervously and clumped tighter. Sven's heart thudded.

Every tale he'd heard of wolves – their long fangs, red eyes and sharp claws – flooded into his mind.

There! Movement in the undergrowth. Sven bent down and fumbled for a stone. His hand trembled as he gripped the cold rock.

A sudden roar burst from the bushes.

"RAAGHH!"

Sven yelped and dropped both the stone and his stick. Two broad-shouldered figures leapt from the shadows, laughing.

"Still scared of the dark, *wolf pup*?" jeered Bjorn, his eldest brother.

His middle brother Torsten doubled over with laughter.

Sven snatched up his stick and turned away. His cheeks burnt hot with shame.

His brothers strode past, smirking. Bjorn carried a large Arctic hare slung over his shoulder.

"Did you catch that?" asked Sven.

Bjorn grunted. "Yup."

"With his bare hands!" added Torsten, grinning.

"Can I come on a hunt with you next time?" pleaded Sven.

Bjorn glanced back. "A hunter needs to be brave – and you're clearly not."

"Best stay here, *wolf pup*!" said Torsten. "Guard the sheep … since you're one of them!"

Laughing, the two brothers headed down the path towards home.

Sven's fists clenched around his stick. He didn't want to be a shepherd. He wanted to be a true Viking. He wanted to wield an axe, not a crook. To cross oceans, not count sheep. As he herded the flock back towards the settlement, he gazed off at the slate-grey sea and dreamt of what lay beyond.

That night, flames danced in the fireplace as the family gathered round for cooked hare and his father's stories. Sven sat in silence, listening but still fuming at his brothers. They'd told their parents about the joke they'd played on their younger *wolf pup*. His father had laughed, while his mother had given him a pitying smile – which was maybe even worse.

Once his father finished telling his tale, talk turned to Leif Erikson – the eldest son of their chieftain Erik the Red, who had founded the Viking settlement in Greenland.

"I hear he's preparing for a voyage west," said their father. "There's a rumour of lands beyond the sea."

"Sounds like he wants to make his name as a great explorer like his father," replied their mother.

"A pointless quest," Bjorn muttered, biting into a strip of meat. "West of Greenland lies only storms and sea monsters."

"Maybe," said their father, as he poked the fire with a stick. "But, supposedly, Bjarni Herjólfsson glimpsed it during a storm that blew his ship off course. It's believed to be a place of endless forests, rich game and warm winds."

"Ha!" snorted Torsten. He tugged his animal skin over his shoulders. "If only."

Their father raised a bushy eyebrow. "Leif is looking for a crew."

"Really? Can I go?" blurted Sven, sitting up.

Both his brothers sniggered.

"Easy there, wolf pup," said his father, with a wry smile. "You're too young."

Bjorn pinched Sven's scrawny bicep. "Leif needs strong arms for the oars, anyway."

"Not scared little sheep boys," teased Torsten.

Sven said nothing.

Later, as the wind howled across the roofs of turf and stone, Sven lay awake, his grey eyes wide with resolve. He wouldn't be mocked any longer.

He would join Leif's crew.

2. Bad omen

The dawn sun cast a golden light across the rippling waters, burning away the last strands of sea mist that clung to the shoreline. At the dock, a crowd had gathered – a mix of fur-cloaked and weather-hardened men and women, and even a few bold youths, all standing in a line beside the longship.

The vessel bobbed with the lapping of waves, its dragon-headed prow carved to scare off sea monsters. Oars jutted from its sides like the legs of a giant water spider. The sail – striped red and white – flapped in the breeze, as if restless to get underway.

Sven stood at the end of the line beside a fish-drying rack. The salty stink of seaweed and smoked cod filled his nostrils. He felt a little jittery and couldn't keep still. This was his chance to leave the sheep behind and become more than just a *wolf pup*.

Leif Erikson stood tall and proud on the dockside. His sandy-red hair and beard shone like polished bronze. A bear-fur cloak hung from his broad shoulders and a seax knife was strapped to his belt.

"This is no voyage for the faint of heart," he announced. His voice rang out like a war horn. "We sail west, to lands only whispered of, where the sea swallows ships, and storms strike like Thor's hammer. But for those brave enough to seek the edge of the world – there will be glory and riches!"

The crowd murmured. Some shifted nervously. Others stepped forward.

Leif walked the line, eyeing each would-be crew member. He tapped a few on the shoulder – seasoned sailors, hardened warriors, skilled hunters, a muscular woman with red hair who claimed she could out-row any man. Then he stopped by a girl in a dark wool tunic. Her pale face was angular and striking, her eyes bluer than the sky, and her ice-blonde hair was braided tight and tied off with a leather cord.

She met his surprised gaze without blinking.

Leif raised an eyebrow. "Aren't you a little young for such a venture?"

The girl didn't flinch. "Aren't you a little old?"

A tense hush fell over the dock.

Then Leif barked out a laugh. "What's your name, girl?"

"Thora."

Leif stroked his beard. "As in … Thora, the great-granddaughter of Aud the Deep-Minded."

The girl nodded.

Leif smiled. "Then that's good enough for me. On board."

Thora marched past him and climbed onto the longship.

Sven's heart quickened as Leif approached closer. But the chieftain's son first paused beside a leathery-skinned man with one eye. "Gamli, what are *you* doing in line?" Leif asked.

"I thought I might be a little *old* for this venture," the man replied, with a wink.

Leif snorted and clapped him on the back. "Of course not. I'd never set sail without you aboard. Now, where's my father?"

"I saw him riding this way," replied Gamli.

"Good." Leif turned to Sven. "Hey lad!"

"Y-yes?" stuttered Sven, straightening to attention.

"What are you standing around for? Get the fish in the hold. We're casting off as soon as my father's here."

Sven's jaw dropped. "I'm coming with you?"

Leif stared at him, confused. "Coming with us? No, lad. My crew's full. You're here to pack the supplies, aren't you? Now move!"

Sven's heart sank like a stone thrown into the fjord.

With a heavy sigh, he bent down and picked up a basket of dried fish at his feet. He trudged over to the longship and across the gangplank. He pushed past a couple of goats tied to the mast and entered the hold. As he stowed the basket, he heard a cry. "Erik the Red has fallen from his horse!"

Everyone turned to see their chieftain limping towards the dock.

"Father, are you hurt?" called Leif.

"I'll live," Erik replied, with a grimace. "But I won't be sailing with you."

"Are you sure, Father?"

"My fall is a bad omen," replied Erik. "Best set off without me."

Sven's pulse quickened. A space had opened up in the crew … he realised it was now or never.

With everyone's attention on their chieftain, Sven ducked into the open hold. He crawled past bundles of dried fish and coils of rope, burrowing himself beneath a mound of animal pelts.

A few moments later, the crew began untying the moorings. The longship creaked as it eased away from the dock. Above, the oars dipped into the water and the longship surged forward.

Sven held his breath. He was on board – bound for the edge of the world.

3. Ship's rat

The longship creaked and groaned as it cut through the waves, oars slapping the sea in a steady rhythm. Sven held his nose as he hid beneath the musty animal skins. He tried not to gag from the stink of damp fur and dried fish. He'd made it on board. There was no turning back now.

After a while, though, he grew cold and stiff. His legs seized up. As he shifted position, the long hairs of an animal skin tickled his nose and made him sneeze. Sven went dead still. He listened hard. The creak of the oars continued.

He let out an unsteady breath and relaxed. He'd got away with it! Then a sudden tug pulled back the skin, letting in a shaft of daylight. A pair of furious blue eyes glared at him.

"I knew I heard a rat," snarled the girl. She wrinkled her nose in disgust. "And smelt one!"

Thora grabbed Sven by the neck of his rough woollen tunic and dragged him out into the open hold. Around them, bundles of dried meat, iron tools and barrels of drinking water clunked with the roll of the ship.

The crew looked up from their oars. A few grunted in surprise. One of them – an old warrior missing half an ear, called Harek – chuckled. "Looks like we've caught ourselves a sea urchin."

Thora shoved Sven forward. "This stowaway was hiding under the furs."

Leif Erikson stood at the prow, his cloak whipping in the wind, his storm-blue eyes narrowed on the horizon. His face was dead set and unreadable.

"He'll slow us down," Thora said, pushing Sven towards the ship's side. "We should throw him overboard and lighten the load."

Sven's heart pounded in his chest. "I can row!" he cried. "I can fish. And I can fight – if I have to."

Leif studied him a moment. "What's your name, lad?"

"Sven."

"Then let's see you row, Sven," said Leif. "But keep up with my crew, or you'll find yourself swimming."

Laughter rippled through the crew as Sven took the spot of another rower and was handed an oar over three times as long as he was tall.

Scowling, Thora leant in close. "Row hard, Rat!" she hissed. "Or I'll feed you to Rán myself."

Sven didn't know if she meant the sea goddess Rán who dragged drowning sailors to the depths – or a crew member with a hungry belly and an even worse temper. Either way, he gritted his teeth and set to rowing.

He had to prove his worth – his life depended on it.

4. Blisters

The wind had died.

The great square sail hung limp from the mast, and the only sound was the groan of wood and the slosh of oars in the water.

Leif ordered the sail to be lowered. Without the help of the wind, every crew member set to rowing – even Leif himself. His sleeves rolled up to the elbow, his powerful arms began working in a steady rhythm.

Sven was not so steady. His hands burnt as he gripped the rough wooden shaft of the oar. His shoulders screamed and his arms felt like they were being pulled from their sockets. Blisters had already formed and each stroke was like dragging fire across his palms.

"Keep up, Rat!" barked Thora, effortlessly pulling her own oar through the water. Her breathing was deep and easy, while Sven gasped like a beached whale.

"How … much … further … do you think?" he panted.

Thora grinned. "You brought this on yourself, Rat. Next time you want to sneak aboard a ship, choose one that doesn't require rowing across half the world."

Sven tried to answer. But at that moment a wave caught his oar. The handle was yanked from his grip and it almost took his head off. The oar clattered against the side of the ship, slowing it down.

"The boy's caught a crab!" complained Harek. "He doesn't know how to row."

"Mark my words," muttered a husky voice from the front. "This boy's the bad omen Erik spoke of."

Sven looked up to see the red-haired woman with arms like tree trunks. Her name was Bryn. She wore a silver amulet of Thor's hammer around her thick neck and rowed with ease, her oar slicing through the waves like a knife.

She glared at Sven. "Erik falls from his horse, and suddenly a stowaway shows up? It's the gods' warning. You'll see."

His cheeks hot with humiliation, Sven picked up his oar and began rowing again. His mouth soon became dry, and his lips cracked. The sun above was harsh, and the salt from the sea and his sweat rubbed raw against his skin. He didn't know how much longer he could keep this up. He'd made a mistake stowing aboard Leif's ship – a very bad mistake.

"Straighten your spine," came a voice from the stern. "Row from the shoulders, not the hands."

Gamli stood at the steerboard, squinting against the glare. His voice was as dry as driftwood. "And wrap your hands, lad. Use this strip of sailcloth, if you want to keep your fingers."

He tossed Sven a length of cloth. Sven caught it and wound the material around his palms. It stung at first, but the rough burn eased. He adjusted his grip on his oar, rolled his shoulders, and tried again.

This time, his oar moved more smoothly. The pain dulled to a throb. He began to find a rhythm.

He could do this. He had to. There was no other choice.

Row or swim, Leif had warned.

Then the sea darkened. A sharp wind swept across the waves, whipping the surface into white-capped peaks. The sky turned steel-grey and thunder rumbled like a battle drum.

"STORM!" Gamli yelled.

5. Thor's hammer

The sea heaved like a writhing serpent. Dark clouds tore across the sky. Thunder boomed and lightning flashed. The storm hit fast, the wind howling in Sven's ears as he rowed for his life.

Then a wall of water smashed into the bow, soaking him to the skin and slamming him sideways on the bench. Another wave pounded the hull. The longship pitched so violently it felt like the monster **_Jörmungandr_** itself was trying to tip them into the sea.

"Thor's hammer is falling hard today!" Gamli yelled from the stern, as he wrestled with the steerboard.

"He must be angry," Bryn called back, "or battling sea serpents again!"

Sven clung desperately to his oar, his arms shaking. All around him, the crew rowed on, their muscles straining, seawater streaming from their beards and hair.

Leif had taken up position at the prow, his bear-fur cloak drenched and flapping behind him. "ROW!" he shouted. "Row or drown!"

Sven dug in. He rowed against the wind. Against the aching pain in his arms. Against the fear that gripped his chest.

He pulled with all the strength he had left. One stroke after another.

A giant wave rose up ahead – taller than the mast, dark as night.

"Hold fast!" Leif roared. "Row into it – don't turn broadside, or we're done for!"

The longship creaked and climbed. Water spilt over the bow. But the ship didn't turn. It didn't capsize. They broke through and rode the wave down.

Moments later, the storm began to ease. The wind softened. The waves shrank. And the sea calmed as suddenly as it had erupted.

The rowers sagged over their oars with exhaustion. Bryn kissed her silver amulet with gratitude.

"Good rowing," said Leif, laying a hand on Sven's soaked shoulder. "Seems you won't be swimming just yet."

Sven let go of the oar and collapsed on the bench. As Leif checked on the rest of his crew, Gamli shot Sven a gap-toothed grin and a wink.

Sven grinned back. But his smile faded when he caught the thunderous look on Thora's face.

"I guess Rán will be going hungry today," she muttered, before turning her back on him.

6. Seaworthy

The wind, at last, was in their favour. With the sail full and the longship slicing through calmer seas, the rowers finally rested.

Sven stretched his aching back and looked out across the rolling blue. Sunlight shimmered on the waves like scattered gold. His clothes were stiff with salt, his hands blistered and his muscles heavy as lead, but there was a fire inside him now. Compared to the rocky terrain of Greenland, he felt like he belonged out here.

Leif watched him a moment, then called to Gamli. "Time the boy learnt something more than rowing."

Gamli stepped away from the steerboard,

handing it over to the grizzled warrior Harek. "Come on, Sven," he said, jerking his head towards the midship. "Let's see if you've got more than fish guts in that skull of yours."

Thora scowled at him as he passed. "Why waste time on a ship's rat?" she muttered.

Sven felt the familiar heat rise in his cheeks. He tried to ignore her, just like he did his brothers.

"Rat or not, he's earned his place," Gamli replied. "Don't forget yours."

His warning silenced her. Sven straightened a little, glad someone was finally on his side.

Gamli set him to work at once. Over the course of the next few days, he showed him how to tie a proper reef knot and a bowline – "One to hold fast, the other to save your life." Then how to mend a tear in the sail with a curved bone needle.

Standing at the stern one morning, Gamli asked Sven to close his eyes.

"Feel the wind," Gamli told him. "Sense its direction. Now adjust the steerboard accordingly."

He taught Sven to read the sea too – to spot ripples that meant shoals of fish or sudden changes in current.

"See the colour shift?" Gamli pointed to a stretch of pale green water. "It's shallower there. Could be rocks underneath. You steer into that, and we're wrecked."

When not working, Sven could relax with the rest of the crew. He played knucklebones and lost many a time at the board game of ***Tafl***. He helped with fishing but kept out of the arm-wrestling competitions. No one could beat Bryn.

One evening, Leif approached him. "You're Askel's boy, aren't you? The sheep herder?"

Sven nodded, worried he was in trouble.

"Then you'll know how to stop the goats eating the ropes," said Leif. "I'm putting you in charge of them." He handed Sven a bucket of dried seaweed and strode off.

Sven sighed. He hadn't quite escaped his shepherding duties. He got to work feeding and tending to the ship's two scrawny goats.

As Sven cleared the dung, Thora strolled over, wrinkling her nose at the smell. "From Rat to Goat Boy," she said, smirking. "Impressive."

Sven glared at her. "What's your problem?"

"You are," she replied bluntly. "You're a bad omen. A danger to this ship and crew."

One of the goats bleated and butted her on the backside.

Sven stifled a laugh as Thora stormed off. At least the goats were on his side.

That night, under a sky filled with stars, Sven couldn't sleep. He found Leif standing alone at the prow, one hand resting upon the long neck of the carved dragon's head. He was staring off at the inky horizon.

"Aren't you scared of falling off the edge of the world?" Sven asked timidly.

"Of course." Leif smiled faintly at the look of shock on Sven's face. "A true Viking fears the edge of the world but sails towards it anyway. Sven, courage isn't the lack of fear – it's rowing on despite that fear."

Sven nodded, thinking he understood the great man's lesson.

Leif pointed to the sky. "You see that star?"

Sven followed his finger. One star burnt brighter than the rest.

"That's *Norðstjarna* – the North Star. It stays where it is, even as the other stars move. We steer by it when the sun is gone, and it's guided sailors home since the dawn of time. Let it guide you."

7. Helluland

Sven was woken by a cry of "LAND!"

Leif Erikson stirred from beneath his cloak and rose. The rest of the crew shrugged off their *húðfat*, the fur-lined sealskins having kept them warm through the night. They clambered to their feet, eyes squinting against the morning mist. Sven stood, yawning, and joined them at the bow.

Through the drifting fog, he saw it too – a dark, jagged coastline. Towering cliffs loomed above a barren shore strewn with great slabs of stone.

He became excited. "Is this it?"

Thora shaded her eyes, a grim expression on her face. "Looks like the end of the world to me."

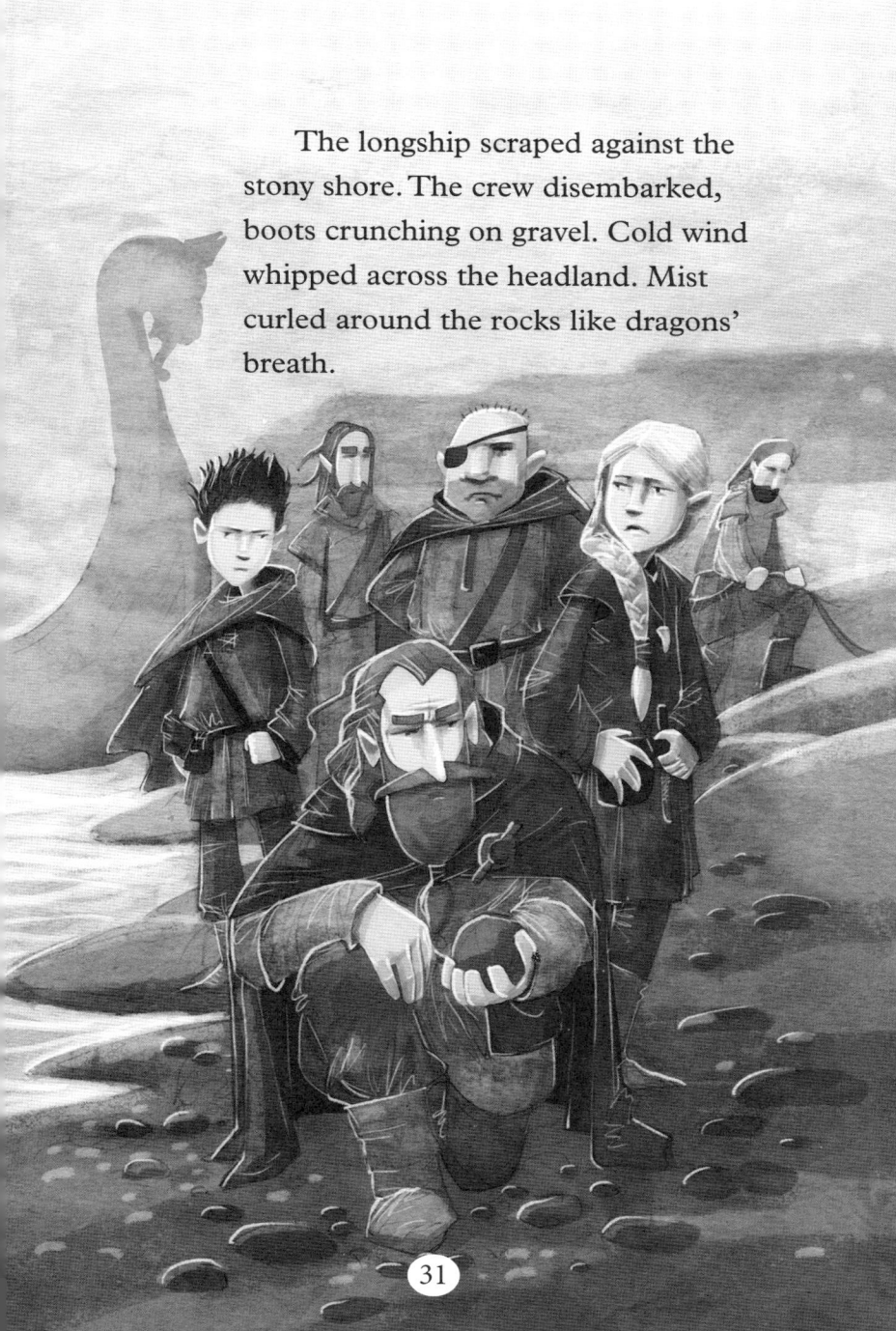

The longship scraped against the stony shore. The crew disembarked, boots crunching on gravel. Cold wind whipped across the headland. Mist curled around the rocks like dragons' breath.

Gamli sniffed the air. "Not much grows here. No trees. No pasture that I can smell."

There was a mutter of discontent among the crew.

Leif knelt and picked up a rock smoothed by the ocean. "I name this place, **Helluland**," he declared. "The Land of Flat Stones."

"No kidding!" moaned Bryn, kicking a large pebble across the stony beach. "Where are the forests? The game? The promised riches?"

Leif discarded the rock and stood up. "Spread out," he ordered. "We need water, food and firewood – if there's any to be found."

The crew split up and began their search. Some picked up bits of driftwood. Others scouted for mussels, seaweed and birds' eggs, while a couple of groups sought out fresh water.

Sven found himself alone with Thora. They each carried an empty goatskin bladder. She walked off, following the trickle of a stream through the rocks. When she reached a rock pool at the base of a cliff, she knelt and tested the water. Satisfied, she began to fill up her bladder. Sven pulled out the stopper of his own bladder.

Thora glanced up angrily. "Hey Rat, find your own stream!"

With a long sigh, Sven wandered away up the beach. As he skirted a mound of boulders, his foot caught on something. Looking down, he gasped. Half-buried in the gravel was a massive, yellowed skull. Its jaw was lined with dagger-like teeth.

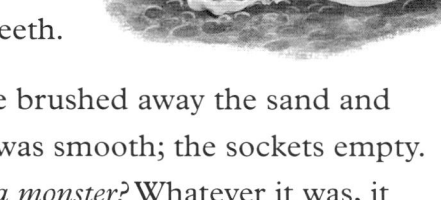

Crouching, he brushed away the sand and gravel. The bone was smooth; the sockets empty. *A polar bear? A sea monster?* Whatever it was, it was terrifying yet thrilling.

As he lifted up the skull, a low growl echoed through the fog. Sven turned sharply, almost dropping the skull. The mist hung like a shroud over the boulders. Another growl. Then a deep, throaty grunt. Something BIG was moving in the gloom. Sven tucked the skull under his arm and fled.

A shadow loomed out of the fog and Sven ran straight into Thora. She dropped her full bladder.

"Hey, watch where you're going!" she snapped. Then she noticed Sven's pale face. "What now, Rat? Lost your tail?"

"I heard something!" he whispered. "Behind the rocks. Growling."

She peered into the mist. "There's nothing there. This place is as dead as that skull in your hands."

"I tell you, I heard something."

"*Scared*, are we?" She smirked. "Maybe you should've stayed at home, sheep boy!"

Sven's fear gave way to fury. She was mocking him, just like his brothers did. Then a long, bone-chilling howl rang out.

Thora's smirk faltered. She spun towards the cliffs. "What kind of creature makes *that* sound?"

Sven didn't wait to find out. Neither did she. They bolted back down the beach. Breathless, they reached the ship. The rest of the crew were gathered in the gloom, eyes wide and weapons out.

"No shellfish. No birds. Not even a scrap of seaweed," muttered Gamli. "This land feeds nothing but ghosts!"

All along the shore, shadows moved in the fog.

"Cast off!" ordered Leif, urging his crew back into the longship.

As Thora climbed aboard, she patted her tunic. "Oh no ... I left my water bladder."

"No time!" barked Leif, his eyes fixed on the misty shore.

The longship slid away from Helluland, its hull scraping against the stones. The crew rowed hard, the wind catching their sail again as they pulled clear of the island.

From the stern, Sven looked back. The land faded into the fog, but the howls still echoed – haunting and hungry. He glanced at the skull beside him. It smelt faintly of rot and of death. A shiver ran down his spine. Courage may well be rowing on, despite the fear – but this time, they were rowing away from that fear.

8. Tempest of Thor

"Good riddance," spat Gamli, adjusting the steerboard as they left Helluland behind.

"Blasted frost giants!" muttered Harek. "Their breath alone turns the land dead."

"And we found nothing but a bit of driftwood!" added Bryn, pulling angrily on her oar. "We're low on supplies now."

The crew rowed in uneasy silence.

Thora glared at Sven, then exploded. "That's your fault, you complete goat-brain!"

Sven blinked. "What did I do this time?"

"You ran into me in the fog. Made me drop my water bladder!" Thora jabbed a finger at the skull at Sven's feet. "Why did you grab *that* instead of filling your water bladder?"

"You wouldn't let me, remember?" Sven shot back. "You told me to find my own stream."

The argument sent murmurs through the crew. Faces turned sour.

"That's because you don't belong in this crew," Thora replied bitterly. "You're a stowaway – "

"ENOUGH!"

All heads turned to the prow. Leif stood steady on the deck, even as the wind tugged at his cloak. "We've supplies enough to last," he said. "And we sail for greener lands."

"How much further are these lands you promise?" challenged a **rune**-faced warrior.

"The wind is with us, Rurik," assured Leif. "So too is **Thor**."

The majority of the crew nodded and resumed rowing, but a few cast worried glances at the black clouds on the horizon.

By dusk, Thor struck. Lightning split the heavens. Thunder rolled. Rain pelted down like sharp needles.

"HOLD FAST!" Leif roared, as the sea heaved and Gamli battled with the steerboard.

A monstrous wave crashed over the longship. *CRACK!* The mast snapped, toppling partway before the ropes caught it. A sailor was struck and knocked over the **gunwale** into the water. Bryn hurled herself across the deck to save him but was too late.

Another surge hit. Thora screamed as she slid across the waterlogged deck.

Sven lunged and grabbed her wrist. "I've got you!" he shouted, bracing his feet against the bench.

Together, they fell back into the shallow of the hold. Thora gaped at him, stunned.

Then *CRUNCH* –

The ship lurched violently.

"We've struck rock!" bellowed Harek. "She's leaking!"

Water poured in through a splintered hole in the hull. The crew scrambled to plug it with spare tunics and tarred rope.

Another wave rolled over the ship, taking with it one of the goats. Several pairs of oars floated away, lost to the waves. Rain pummelled them. The wind howled like the monstrous wolf Fenrir himself, tearing at their cloaks and their spirit.

"This is Thor's wrath," cried the grey-bearded Haldor, his eyes wild. "We angered the Thunderer!"

"No!" Leif growled. "This is Thor's *test*. The storm is his hammer – let's prove we're forged strong enough to survive it!"

But hope was wearing as thin as the sailcloth.

Sven clung to the broken mast, soaked and shivering. Fear gripped his heart. He thought of his mother and father, of warm fires and dry land.

He was going to drown in this icy sea. Still, if this was Thor's tempest, he would face it like a true Viking. Gritting his teeth, he stood and turned to the wind just as another wave engulfed him …

9. Sea monster

Sven awoke with a start. His clothes hung off him like seaweed, cold and limp. He was lying in a pool of water at the bottom of the longship.

The storm had passed.

The sky above was a clear blue. The sea stretched glassy and calm in every direction. The crew lay scattered and motionless across the deck, like driftwood cast upon the shore. Even Leif was still and silent, having tied himself to the dragon-headed prow. He dangled over the water, a figurehead to Viking courage.

But beneath the stillness lurked danger. The hull creaked and groaned – more than usual.

Sven sat up. He remembered … *The ship was leaking!* He scrambled to the side, where a soaked mass of rope and torn cloth had been jammed into a jagged hole. Water still trickled through. He tried to pack the hole with more cloth, but it just squelched out uselessly.

"You'll drown us quicker doing it like that," said Thora, kneeling down beside him.

Sven braced for the insult. But instead, she took out a tar pot and a strip of wool. "Like this," she said, forcing the wool deep, then smearing tar over it with practised hands. "Wool holds. Tar seals."

"Got it," said Sven. As Thora plugged the hole, he grabbed a bucket and started bailing.

Thora glanced at him. "I guess you're not *completely* useless."

Sven couldn't help but grin. For Thora, that was practically a compliment.

The leak slowed, but the damage was done.

As the crew stirred, the worry spread. The ship was slowly sinking. Vital supplies had been lost.

One of the goats was gone, the other bleating miserably. And two members of the crew were missing.

"We're doomed," murmured Haldor, tugging fitfully at his grey beard.

Then a ripple disturbed the glassy sea. A moment later, the water around the longship churned.

"***Draugr!***" Harek gasped in horror. "The drowned dead have come for us."

Bryn looked over the side. A black fin sliced the surface. "No, it's a sea monster!"

A huge, dappled shape surged beneath the hull; its dorsal fin was as tall as a man. It rammed the side. The longship shuddered.

"The goddess Rán sends her beast to drag us down!" cried Svala, a salty-haired woman with hands toughened by rope and oar.

"No, not us," snarled Bryn. "She sends it for *him*!" She pointed an accusing finger at Sven. "The stowaway. The bad omen."

Others turned, their eyes dark and full of fear.

"I'm not – " Sven began, but Haldor stepped forward.

"Erik the Red foresaw it in his fall. This boy brings misfortune."

"Feed him to the sea monster," growled another. "Spare the rest of us."

The crew surrounded Sven. They would sacrifice the boy to save themselves.

10. Adrift

Sven retreated to the stern. He had nowhere to go.

"Throw him overboard!" yelled Haldor, his face twisted in fury.

Several crew members surged towards Sven. He saw Thora rise, uncertain. Gamli shouted something, but his words were lost among the noise.

Then the longship rocked violently as the sea monster rammed it again. Some of the sailors lost their footing. More water poured in through the split in the hull. The monster dived and circled round for another attack.

"Hurry!" ordered Haldor. "Before the beast comes back."

Rough hands seized Sven. He struggled, his heart pounding, as they pushed him to the rail.

"BY THOR'S HAMMER, STOP!"

Leif now stood on the deck, his face like thunder, the rope in his hand like a whip. "Let him go."

"He's a bad omen!" argued Haldor.

"He's but a boy," replied Leif.

Hands loosened on Sven's tunic and he shook himself free. Behind him, the sea monster's fin cut through the water like a blade.

"The ship won't take another hit," said Rurik.

"We must appease the gods!" cried Bryn. She lunged for Sven.

Desperate, Sven grabbed one of the last intact oars from the deck, brandishing it like a staff.

"Stay back!" he warned, swinging the oar as the crew closed in.

"The rat's got a stick now," Bryn sneered. But before she could disarm him, the monster breached the surface. It rose from the water, a black and white mountain of muscle, blubber and sharp teeth.

"Brace yourselves!" yelled Haldor, dropping to the deck.

Sven didn't hesitate. He turned and struck the beast square on the nose with his oar.

CRACK! The oar snapped in two. The sea monster twisted its great bulk away from the ship. Then, with a slap of its tail, the creature sent a wave crashing over the gunwale before disappearing into the depths.

A stunned silence followed. Only the creak of the damaged hull and the ragged breathing of the crew broke the stillness.

Sven stood frozen, the broken oar clenched in his fists. His arms trembled. He wasn't sure if it was from fear or the thrill of battling a sea monster ... and living to tell the tale.

Gamli was the first to speak. "By Thor's beard ... well struck." He went over and gave Sven a solid clap on the back that nearly knocked him over.

Thora eyed the snapped oar in his hand, then met his gaze. "You're stronger than you look, Goat Boy."

Sven managed a weak smile. Her words weren't exactly warm – but neither were they cruel.

Leif approached last, nodding slowly.

"You just saved this ship, Sven. And all our lives with it. You've earned your place in my crew."

Sven lowered the broken oar, a sense of pride warming his heart. For the first time, he felt like a true Viking.

Then his blood ran cold at the sight of his fellow Vikings. They stood shoulder to shoulder, arms crossed and their expressions fierce.

"You *don't* have a crew," muttered Haldor, scowling through his long grey beard. "Leif, you don't even have a ship."

Leif turned to see his own crew standing against him.

"The hull is split!" shouted Rurik.

"The mast's cracked clean through!" said Harek.

"And we've lost another oar!" Bryn added angrily.

Sven gazed around. The sail hung in tatters. The remaining oars were few and uneven. The sea was flat, and there wasn't a breath of wind.

They were adrift.

11. Mutiny

The longship floated on a sea of glass. The sky above blazed with a cruel sun. No wind. No sail. No land in sight.

The crew were restless. Angry murmurs rippled up and down the benches like a growing wave. A few rowed with the remaining oars, while the others threw seawater off the boat.

"We're drifting to our deaths," muttered Haldor, his thick brows crossed. "We should turn back."

Svala hunted through the meagre supplies in the hold. "We're running out of food and water," she moaned, holding up an empty goatskin bladder.

"Ration it," ordered Leif.

"There's barely enough for half the crew!" she snapped. "And we can't eat wood."

"Then we'll fish," Leif replied.

Bryn snorted. "Does Sven plan to conjure up another sea monster to feed us? Maybe we can use him as bait?"

A few sailors chuckled darkly.

Sven kept his distance. He crouched beside the patched hole in the hull, looking out at the endless horizon. The monster was gone. But the real danger had only just begun.

The crew was split. Haldor, Bryn and Harek and most of the crew were on one side. Leif, Gamli, a few loyal seamen and Sven … plus, surprisingly, Thora were on the other.

Leif stood tall beside the broken mast, his hand resting on the hilt of his seax knife. His eyes scanned the mutinous crew. "I promised new lands," he said. "And I do not break my word."

"Your word won't fill our bellies," growled Haldor.

"Or fix our ship," said Rurik.

"Until the boy is gone, this voyage is cursed," muttered Bryn, holding up her silver amulet of Thor's hammer against Sven.

Leif glared at her. "If Thor tests us, we pass by rowing harder and working together, *not* sacrificing each other." He pointed at Sven. "This boy faced the sea monster while the rest of you stood frozen or cowered on the deck. If that's not Viking courage, what is?"

Some shifted guiltily. Others looked away. Sven felt another rush of pride.

"There's courage," replied Haldor. "And then there's recklessness."

Thora stepped forward, her face flushed from sun and fury. "Better to die seeking greatness than crawl home with our tails between our legs!"

Haldor scowled. "And what would you know of greatness? You live off the fame of your ancestor. You're nothing but a vain, glory-seeking girl."

Thora reached for her sheath. "You want to test me, Haldor?"

Haldor stood and drew his axe. Gamli raised a hand to calm them, but the tension crackled like lightning.

Then Leif spoke again, his voice cutting through the fragile moment. "We all have our reasons for being on this voyage. I ask for three more days. By Thor's hand, he will deliver us."

Haldor lowered his axe. "*One* more day," he growled. "But if your miracle land doesn't appear, we turn east. Back to Greenland."

That one day passed slowly. The sun beat down. Lips cracked. Thirst gnawed at every throat. Sven's head ached, his stomach had cramps and his tongue felt like leather.

The lone goat bleated weakly, knowing its hours were numbered.

As the sun dipped low, their hopes sank with it.

The crew gathered again, words and weapons sharpened.

"Leif, it's time you handed over command of this ship," said Haldor, axe in hand.

Leif stood defiant, clasping the hilt of his knife. "Just another day. That's all we need."

"This is pointless," snapped Rurik. "We're all going to –"

"LAND!" came a cry from the prow.

Heads snapped around.

On the distant horizon was a dark green line – trees. A whole forest.

For a moment, Sven thought it was a mirage. Then a flock of birds flew overhead on their way to roost in the trees.

Leif smiled, his grip relaxing on his seax knife. "Thor tested us – and we did not turn back."

Shaking his head in wonder, Gamli gave a wheezy chuckle. "Lucky, Leif, very lucky."

12. Markland

Leif jumped from the longship onto the beach, his boots sinking into the wet sand. As he strode up to the edge of the forest, Sven and the rest of the crew followed in his footprints.

As far as the eye could see, towering trees reached skyward, lush, green and full of life. The air was sweet with pine and the promise of survival.

Leif pressed a hand to the trunk of a tall fir tree, as if blessing it. "**Markland**," he declared. "Land of Forests."

A ragged cheer burst from the crew. After weeks of hardship, fear and near mutiny, they had land beneath their feet and hope in their hearts.

Buckets and water bladders were filled with cold, fresh water from a nearby stream. The goat was led ashore to graze. Fires were lit for cooking. The last of the salted meat was shared, and even the flint-hearted Haldor cracked a smile when Gamli caught a salmon with his bare hands.

The next morning, Sven and Thora were sent to search the forest for berries and mushrooms. They walked in silence, the sound of birdsong filling the space between them.

At a stream, Thora bent to fill her new water bladder, then glanced up when Sven hesitated on the far side of the bank. "What are you waiting for?" she asked.

Sven offered a strained smile. "I thought you wouldn't want me sharing your stream."

She straightened. "Be my guest."

Sven crouched down and pulled out the stopper of his own bladder. As he dipped it in the stream, Thora quietly said, "You saved me. In the storm. Thanks."

Sven shrugged. "You'd have done the same."

Thora didn't reply right away. "Maybe – "

Sven raised an eyebrow. "Maybe?"

Thora swallowed hard. "It would've been one way to get rid of my rival," she admitted.

"*Rival?*" Sven stood and stared at her. "What makes you think I'm your rival?"

"You snuck on board to take my place, my glory," Thora replied. "You want to be the youngest explorer."

"What? No!" replied Sven. "I just wanted to escape my brothers and prove to my family I'm not some scared little sheep boy! Not a … wolf pup!"

"Oh – " said Thora, lowering her gaze to the ground. "Sorry, I guess I just felt a bit threatened by you, that's all."

"Threatened by *me*? Why?" asked Sven.

Thora turned to a cranberry bush and began picking its fruit. "It isn't easy. Living up to such expectations."

Sven blinked. "What expectations?"

"Aud the Deep-Minded was my great-grandmother. She led her people across the sea. Founded a settlement in Iceland. Was respected by kings and warriors. That's why I'm here – trying to live up to her legend." Thora plucked a bright red berry from a branch. "But ... sometimes I feel like I have to battle everyone to prove I'm worthy of her legacy."

Sven shook his head slowly. "Thora, you're strong, clever and fearless in your own right. You just don't need to be mean to prove it."

Thora looked up guiltily. "I'm sure my great-grandmother wasn't mean. Sorry."

She tossed him the berry.

Sven caught it and popped it into his mouth. "Apology accepted," he said, with a grin.

They both set to picking the fruit, working together in silence, as friends.

Over the next few weeks, the crew laboured like true craftspeople. Axes were swung and trees were felled. They repaired the hull with fresh wood, tarred and sealed the gaps, carved new oars and even fashioned a mast stronger than before. Spirits soared with each stroke of the axe and each swing of the hammer.

Then, one evening, as they gathered around the fire, Leif addressed his crew. "This land is good," he said. "But not the one spoken of. I believe there are richer lands to the south. Greener shores, with pasture. A place where we can truly settle."

Haldor rose. "We've worked hard. We've survived. Prospered even. And now you ask us to risk it all again?"

Leif nodded. "We're close. I feel it in my bones. We must press on, to the edge of the world."

13. The edge of the world

As they left Markland's lush forests behind, Leif took up position at the prow. He fixed his gaze on the horizon ahead. Behind him, the crew rowed with reluctant strokes of their new oars.

"We had everything we needed," Bryn growled. "Why tempt the fate of the gods?"

"There was timber enough to make us all rich!" muttered Rurik.

Haldor glared at the back of Leif's head. "Pride drives us now. Not sense."

Three days passed. As they crossed open waters, the longship creaked and moaned as much as the crew. But the wind slowly turned soft and warm. The harsh chill of the north faded, replaced by something fresher and sweeter. Even the sea itself changed – it became bluer, calmer, as if it too was tired of storms.

Then, at dawn on the fourth day, a new land appeared on the horizon. Sven scrambled to his feet and joined Leif at the prow.

The ship drifted into a sheltered bay. Birds wheeled overhead. Rolling grassland led to a forest. Wild vines snaked over rocks and trunks, heavy with ripe, purple grapes. A herd of reindeer bounded along the tree line, startled by their arrival. The air was warm and scented, unlike any place they'd come across before.

Leif leapt ashore. "This is it," he breathed. "The land of legend."

He picked a grape from a vine and took a bite. As the juice burst on his lips, he turned to his crew, his eyes shining with delight. "**Vinland**! Land of the Vines!"

A cheer erupted from the crew. All doubts and fears forgiven and forgotten. They had made it.

They'd found the fabled land.

Gamli clapped his captain on the back. "Leif the Lucky strikes again!"

Leif set his crew to work. Trees were felled. Timber cut. Soon, sturdy longhouses rose from the earth, their walls built of logs and their roofs thatched with turf. The dwellings were just like those back in Greenland, but these were warmer, cosier.

The crew named the place *Leifsbúðir* – Leif's camp.

Sven and Thora helped raise beams, dig fire pits, hunt reindeer and gather grapes. They worked until their arms ached, but neither complained. This new settlement was the fruits of their labour. A new Viking settlement.

One evening, as the fires crackled and laughter echoed through the camp, Sven found himself beside Thora on the grass, a plate of roast reindeer in his lap, a satisfied smile on his face.

Thora nudged him. "You've changed, *wolf pup*."

"Hey!" He frowned. "Not a wolf pup anymore."

"No," she agreed. "All that grape picking has done you the world of good!" She popped a fresh grape in her mouth and laughed. So did Sven.

As the laughter died away, he gazed around the camp, at his fellow crew by the fire, the longhouses and out over the bay.

He had crossed the iron-grey sea. Faced storms, beasts, hunger and fear. He had stood his ground when they tried to throw him overboard. And he'd defeated a sea monster single-handedly.

He was no longer the youngest brother shepherding a flock of scrawny sheep.

He was a Viking explorer.

Setting aside his plate, Sven lay back in the grass, full and content, the heat of the fire at his feet. Above him stretched a sky clearer than he'd ever seen, the stars sharp and bright.

And there it was – *Norðstjarna*. The North Star. The same star that had guided his clan to Greenland. The same star that had guided them to this fine land. Sven smiled to himself. He'd made it. They had sailed to the edge of the world. And found something even greater. A new life.

14. Tracks

Sven's sense of peace and contentment still lingered the next morning. The dawn sunlight shone warm and golden. Dew glistened in the grass. Birds sang from the treetops, their chorus sweet and gentle in his ears.

Thora led the hunt that morning, her bow and arrow in hand, her eyes alert. Sven walked beside her, carrying a wooden spear and watching her every move.

She crouched low beside a patch of grass and pointed to a fresh set of Y-shaped tracks in the dirt. "Grouse," she whispered. "Close by."

Sven nodded. A thrill ran through him. His brothers had *never* let him join their hunts.

Together, they crept through the undergrowth. Thora signalled with quick flicks of her fingers. Sven followed, stepping where she stepped and listening for the faintest rustle. She indicated for him to go left. He edged silently around a large bush. Then, on Thora's signal, he disturbed the bush with his spear.

There was a *squawk!* When the bird broke cover, Thora didn't hesitate. She let loose her arrow. It struck true.

Sven let out a low whistle. "You made that look easy," he said.

Thora slung her bow across her back. "It's not." She picked up the grouse and handed it to him. "Takes teamwork."

Sven carried the grouse with pride. But as they headed back to camp, Thora suddenly stopped and shot a hand to block him.

"What is it?" he asked.

She pointed to the soft earth. "New tracks."

There, pressed into the dirt, was a pair of footprints – small and narrow.

"An elf?" Sven whispered, only half-joking.

"Maybe," Thora replied, her eyes narrowing, "or else – " She trailed off.

A *snap* of a branch made them both spin around. They scanned the forest, but it was still. Too still. Thora and Sven hurried back to camp and told Leif.

"Footprints, you say. Did you see anyone?" he asked.

They both shook their heads.

"And you're certain they weren't your own?"

"Too small," replied Thora. "And barefoot. No turnshoe print."

Leif stroked his beard thoughtfully. "Let's keep this to ourselves for the moment. We don't want to alarm the rest of the crew."

That night, Sven couldn't sleep. The thought of the footprint played on his mind. As he stepped outside to get some air, he stopped dead in his tracks.

Under the glow of the full moon, an object sat on the earth before him.

A carved wooden figure.

It stood no taller than his hand. Its body was blocky, but the face had sharp features – a long nose, wide eyes and teeth bared in a grin that wasn't quite friendly. Feathers were tied around its neck and red paint streaked its face.

Sven stared at it. He shivered as a cool breeze rustled the leaves in the forest. "Thora," he hissed, backing into the longhouse. "You need to see this."

Soon, the whole crew had gathered. The figure was sitting in the centre of them all like an uninvited guest.

"What is it?" asked Sven.

"A spirit marker," replied Gamli, his voice tight.

"Or a trick from the gods?" suggested Rurik.

Leif crossed his arms, meeting the totem's gaze. "Thora and Sven found footprints on their hunt this morning," he revealed.

An uneasy murmur rippled through the crew.

Haldor grimaced. "We've trespassed on cursed ground. It's a warning!"

"No," said Leif, firmly. "This isn't a curse. But someone – or something – is watching us."

"Watching?" muttered Bryn, gripping the hilt of her axe. "Or waiting?"

Leif shook his head slowly. "If they wanted to attack us, they'd not be leaving gifts."

Thora cocked her head to one side and studied the grinning wooden figure. "But is it a gift?"

Leif swept his gaze along the tree line.

"They're watching to see how we answer. Gamli, leave out a jug of goat's milk."

Harek snorted. "*Goat's milk?* We're Vikings. We should answer with iron!"

"Even a bear offers its paw before it strikes," replied Leif. "Let them see our hand is open … not armed. But from now on, keep weapons close. Fires burning. And eyes sharp."

As they settled back to bed, Sven felt the warmth of Vinland turn chill.

The forest was no longer silent.

It was alive, watching and listening.

15. First contact

When they emerged the next morning, the jug of goat's milk was empty.

There'd been no sound or sign of who had taken it. But the lid had been placed back on the stone, as if in thanks.

Thora glanced at Sven. "Best get milking the goat," she said, with a smirk.

Around the camp, the usual rhythm of work began, although every Viking kept one eye on the woods.

Thora and Svala inspected the fishing nets, repairing torn strands with bone needles. Haldor stoked the fire pit while Bryn pounded iron rivets flat for arrowheads. Gamli and Rurik worked the forge bellows, heating metal for the ship repairs. Leif paced the settlement, checking the longhouse roofs and the wooden fence they'd begun to raise from pointed stakes.

Once he'd finished milking the goat, Sven helped Harek sharpen a blade, but his hands trembled as he tried to hold the **whetstone** steady.

"Do you think they'll come again? At night?" asked Sven, unable to shake the uneasy feeling of being watched.

Harek shrugged. "Whether friend or foe, we'll find out soon enough." He held the blade up to the light and ran a finger along its edge. "And I'll be ready for them."

The day passed slowly, the tension stretching out like a taut sail. Then, as the sun dipped low and shadows crept across the grass, a sharp whistle pierced the calm.

"Movement in the trees!" warned Bryn, getting to her feet.

The Vikings dropped their tools and grabbed weapons. A dozen figures stepped from the forest – swift and painted in clay and ash. They held wooden spears and bows with arrows, and their earth-brown eyes were watchful and wary.

The forest held its breath.

Leif raised up a hand, palm open. "We mean no harm," he said slowly, then tapped his chest. "Leif. Viking."

A tall figure among the newcomers stepped forward. His hair was braided with bone beads, he wore a cloak of reindeer skins, and his skin was marked with swirling red paint.

Leif motioned to the milk jug, now full. "Trade?" he asked, pointing from himself to them and miming an exchange.

After a tense pause, two baskets of berries and two skinned rabbits were laid gently on the grass.

A trade was made.

Hesitant smiles exchanged.

As they stood in uncertain silence, Sven noticed a young warrior eyeing his polar bear skull, which hung outside the longhouse. He was gazing at it with a mix of fear and awe.

Sven made a decision. He took down the skull and presented it to the young warrior.

The boy blinked in surprise, then accepted it with reverence. In return, he offered his carved bone amulet – shaped like the head of a deer – and handed it to Sven.

Their eyes met.

No words passed between them. But something shifted in the two groups' attitude.

Hope. *Friendship even?*

The visitors to their camp retreated to the forest, not once turning their backs. As the last melted into the trees, Gamli let out a long breath and loosened his grip on his knife. "Good ... that went well."

Leif nodded. "Today, yes. Let's hope tomorrow's the same."

16. Fire and fear

It was Haldor who first called them "pelt-wearers" for they were cloaked head to toe in soft animal skins, unlike the Vikings with their rough-spun wool and linens.

Cautious trade continued between them through summer and into autumn. Each side remained wary, yet curiosity and a desire to barter kept the peace. The Vikings offered fish, woven cloth and forged iron nails. In return, the locals brought fresh game, walrus tusks and reindeer hides.

Sven and Thora were among the few who seemed at ease with the strangers. They began to recognise faces, gestures – even names. The young warrior who'd given Sven the carved bone talisman came often with the hunters. Called Teyo by his people, he had piercing eyes and a quiet strength.

Together, the three explored the edge of the woods, exchanged words and knowledge, and compared skills. Teyo showed them how to walk silently through the trees and how to spot the tracks of foxes in the frost. Thora shared the art of fire-making with flint and steel, while Sven taught Teyo how to milk a goat.

Teyo was like the supportive brother Sven had always wanted. Thora delighted in besting them both in hunting and games of *Tafl*. And, for his part, Teyo was impressed by Thora's hunting skills and fascinated by her ice-blonde hair.

Their friendship grew like the changing forest – bright and hopeful in the blaze of autumn. But Sven noticed how quickly those golden leaves turned brittle and began to fall.

Then, as winter approached, the peace cracked like ice.

It began with a simple trade – a reindeer hide in exchange for five arrowheads. But something was miscounted, or misunderstood. Voices were raised. Harek stood up, his axe high, and accused one of the pelt-wearers of stealing an arrowhead. The warrior tensed, drawing his knife. The rest of his tribe raised their bows. The crew grabbed their axes and spears.

Leif shoved between them. "Weapons down! Now!"

For a moment, no one moved. Then, slowly, both sides stepped back.

The trade ended in tense silence. But the damage was done. Trust broken.

That night, a shout tore through the camp. "Fire!" yelled Rurik. "The store's alight!"

Flames licked the walls of one of the storage huts. Buckets of seawater and sand were thrown, but it was too late. The roof collapsed in a spray of embers.

"The pelt-wearers!" growled Harek. "They burnt it!"

"You don't know that," Sven argued.

"It could've been an accident," insisted Thora. "A knocked-over lantern, a spark from the forge – "

"No Viking would set fire to their own buildings!" snapped Haldor.

"And Teyo would never do such a thing either," Thora shot back.

Haldor glared at her and Sven. "You two are becoming too familiar with the pelt-wearers. It's clouding your judgement."

"We should strike before they do any worse," said Bryn, punching a fist into her palm.

Leif's eyes narrowed, his face grim in the flickering firelight. "Strike, and we may start a battle we can't win – not without more warriors, at least."

"We're Vikings!" bellowed Harek, holding his blade aloft. "We're born to win!"

As the crew argued, Sven stood silent beside Thora, the heat of the fire warming one side of his face, the cold night air biting the other. He felt the same in his heart – caught between the warmth of new friendship and the chill of steel being drawn.

Trust had melted like snow in spring. And something far more dangerous now hung in the air. Fear.

17. Hunting accident

Winter came. It wasn't as cruel and chilling to the bone as in Greenland, but it was still cold and bitter. Frost silvered the ground, rivers stiffened with ice, and the trees stood brittle and bare. The camp huddled together for warmth, but the bond between the Vikings and the pelt-wearers had frozen over.

Distrust led to hostility. Trade trickled to a stop. And there were no more visits from Teyo, or his tribe. Only shadows and silence filled the forest now.

Both Sven and Thora felt the loss of their friend.

As the snow fell, food grew scarce. Their stores were low. Hunting became vital.

One morning, Harek returned with blood on his spear and a troubled look in his eyes. Both Bryn and Haldor were strangely quiet.

Leif greeted them at the door to the longhouse. "Good hunting?"

"Not exactly," muttered Haldor.

Leif glanced at the blood on the blade. "But you speared something? What was it?"

When they didn't answer, Leif's face paled. "What have you done?"

"He wore furs," Harek said, with a shrug. "Moved like a deer."

Thora gasped in shock. "You hurt a pelt-wearer?"

Bryn stepped in. "He thought it was prey. A mistake."

Leif nodded gravely. "Yes, it certainly was a mistake."

The next day, the tribe came.

They appeared silently through the snow.
Silent. Swift. A line of pelts and painted faces.
Teyo was among them, his face tight with rage.
Behind him, bows were drawn, spears ready.

Leif stepped forward, arms raised. "Peace!"

Sven and Thora joined him, their hearts pounding.

"Teyo!" Thora called. "Accident. A mistake in the woods."

Teyo said nothing. He looked not at Thora, but straight at Harek.

Sven clutched the talisman around his neck. "*Please*," he said, his voice cracking, "we didn't mean for this to happen."

Teyo gestured with his hands then held up his bow and arrow. His meaning was clear – the pelt-wearers wanted the Vikings to leave.

Haldor scoffed. "You dare threaten us!"

"Haldor – " Leif warned.

But Harek had already stepped forward, spear in hand. "If it's a fight you want," he growled, "I'll give it."

"NO!" Gamli shouted, trying to wrestle the spear from him.

But it was too late. An arrow flew. Then another. Chaos broke out.

Sven dropped to the ground. Arrows thudded into the thick snow and wooden walls of the longhouse. Then came a cry – a deep, familiar one – and Gamli collapsed, an arrow lodged in his chest.

"Gamli!" Leif shouted, racing to his side.

But it was no use. Gamli's eye had already turned skywards. He was with the gods, feasting in **Valhalla**.

Moments later, the pelt-wearers melted back into the forest.

Silence fell, snowflakes forming a white shroud over Gamli's body.

Sven's hands trembled. The man who'd first stood up for him, who'd taught him to tie knots, feel the wind and read the sea, now lay still. And the world felt colder for it.

Leif knelt beside his fallen friend. His face crumpled, but no tears came. Only fire in his eyes.

"We'll find no peace here after what has happened. We leave," he said, his voice low but certain. "At the first thaw." No one argued.

The days dragged by. The longhouse felt emptier without Gamli's jokes and booming laughter. Even Thora turned silent and sullen. Sven caught her sharpening her blade late one night, her face set like flint.

When spring's breath finally melted the snow, the Vikings packed their belongings. They filled the open hold with animal hides and timber and stocked up for the long voyage.

Before they left, Sven dug a small hole in the thawing earth. He placed the carved talisman – the gift from Teyo – into the soil where Gamli had fallen. A farewell to both.

The longship pushed off. Oars cut through the frigid water and Vinland faded into a grey mist. They had come to the edge of the world in hope. They left in sorrow and silence. Whether any Viking would ever return, Sven didn't know. But he knew the welcome would no longer be warm.

18. The eye of the storm

With the longship loaded with thick furs, walrus tusks and enough timber to build a small village, the return voyage should have felt victorious. But every oar stroke felt like a tug of defeat. Not one of the crew smiled. No songs were sung. Gamli's absence left a void that not even the ocean could fill.

Harek now stood in his place at the steerboard. He hadn't spoken since the moment Gamli fell. He was a shadow of the warrior he once was. No one challenged him. They didn't need to. The guilt hung around his shoulders heavier than any anchor.

As they sailed across the iron-grey sea, the clouds ahead turned black as pitch.

A deep rumble rolled across the sky. Lightning flashed – not once, but three times in quick succession.

"The gods are angry," growled Haldor.

"This storm – " said Rurik, turning his face towards Harek, "it's for the killing of that warrior."

Leif gritted his teeth. "Then we'll pay for it in hard rowing and rough seas! Now row, all of you!"

The crew obeyed, muscles straining as wind and rain lashed at their backs. The waves rose higher, white-tipped beasts crashing over the side. Thunder boomed like a war hammer. The mast groaned. The sail flailed. Still, they pushed onwards.

Then the storm struck with all its fury.

Lightning speared the sky and struck the steerboard. Harek cried out. For a moment, he glowed like the fire of *Muspelheim* – then he was gone, into the foaming sea.

As the longship turned broadside to the waves, Leif lunged for the steerboard. But too late. A monstrous wave surged over the deck. It hit like a giant's fist and swept him overboard. Terror gripped the crew. They lost their rhythm. Even Bryn dropped her oar.

"The gods have judged us!" she cried. "Harek struck. Now Leif's gone too!"

"We're all doomed!" moaned Haldor, tugging at his long grey beard.

"NO!" shouted Thora, her blue eyes fierce. "Not while we still draw breath."

Without hesitation, she seized the steerboard. She braced herself like a tree in a storm, as the next wave approached.

"ROW!" she bellowed. "NOW!"

The crew obeyed, more from fear than faith. The longship met the wave head-on and rose up and over its white peak. Thora steered them through the storm like she was born to do it.

Sven sprinted to the stern. Rain lashed his face. "LEIF!" he screamed into the storm.

A flash of white foam, a wave of an arm – then a voice, faint but real: "Help!"

Sven grabbed a rope, tied it with a reef knot to the stern and the other end with a bowline to an oar. Gamli's knots – the ones he'd taught him – "One to hold fast, the other to save your life."

He hurled the oar into the sea. "Leif, grab it!" he shouted.

Waves rose and fell. The oar dragged behind the longship. Then – a hand. Leif's fingers found the oar and he looped the bowline around his chest.

"He's got it!" cried Sven.

The crew hauled him in, hand over hand. Leif collapsed onto the deck, half-drowned … but alive. Sven slapped him hard on the back as he threw up a lungful of seawater.

"Leif the Lucky strikes again!" said Sven, smiling, as he recalled Gamli's words.

19. Shipwrecked

Thunder rumbled far behind them. The wind calmed and the waves settled. The storm was over – but it had left its scars.

The longship **listed** slightly to starboard. Rigging hung in frayed tangles. The sail was torn. Oars were cracked. And while the hull had held, water sloshed ankle-deep in the hold.

But, if the boat was in a bad way, Leif was in an even worse state. Covered by a thick fur cloak, he lay unconscious beneath the stars. His skin was as pale as the moonlight and his lips were tinged blue.

"Do you think he'll live?" asked Haldor.

Svala laid a hand on Leif's forehead.

She nodded. "He's ice-cold, but he's as strong as a bear. Give him time."

"I guess the gods didn't completely abandon us," said Bryn, wearily.

"I don't know about that," Rurik replied, gazing around at the ruined longboat. "We may not be dead, but we've yet to escape *Jörmungandr*'s grip."

The exhausted crew slumped where they lay, surrendering to their fate.

Sven realised Leif had been their compass, their anchor and their sail. Without him, the crew began to drift – not just across the sea, but into despair.

Sven turned to Thora. "We have to do something."

She shrugged. "Like what?"

"You're the great-granddaughter of Aud the Deep-Minded," he reminded her. "Take command!"

Thora blinked, hesitated, then strode across the deck and took up Leif's position at the prow.

The crew stared at her blankly.

"Leif gave everything to take us to the edge of the world," she told them. "Now we must give everything to get him home. So, start getting the water out! Fix the sail and lines! And row!"

No one moved. Thora's face hardened to stone. "NOW!" she yelled.

Her voice cut through the night like a battle cry. Shaken out of their stupor, the crew set to work.

Sven took hold of the steerboard. Briefly, he closed his eyes, remembering the firm grip of Gamli's hand guiding his, as the sailor explained wind angles, currents and the sounds of the sea.

"Let the wind be at your back," Gamli had said, "and always watch the water – its colour will tell you where's safe to sail and where danger lurks."

A sad smile touched Sven's lips at the memory.

Now it was up to him. He glanced at the night sky. There was *Norðstjarna* – the star that never moved.

"Follow the North Star and you'll find home," Leif had told him.

Sven trimmed the sail just enough to catch the wind without snapping the weakened mast.

They made slow but steady progress. Then, on the third day, Thora spotted something. "Wreckage!" she shouted from the prow.

Bits of decking and a snapped oar bobbed on the swell. A shredded sail flapped on a rocky isle ahead. Cries echoed faintly across the waves.

"Survivors!" Thora turned to Sven. "Bring us in behind the rocks. Portside!"

Sven nodded, his eyes sharp on the water's surface. He watched for colour shifts – blue for deep, green and brown for shallows, black where jagged rocks lurked below.

With a deft touch on the tiller, he guided the ship through a narrow channel of calmer water. The crew nodded to each other in awe at his skill.

On Thora's command, ropes were thrown to the rocky isle. One by one, the stranded men – a Viking fishing crew – were pulled aboard. One had a broken leg. Another a gash to the head.

"You're lucky we found you," said Haldor, as Svala offered them furs, food and tended to their wounds.

"No," said one of the rescued men. "You're the lucky ones – to have a girl like her in command."

He held a fist to his chest and bowed his head in respect to Thora.

20. Sea Wolf

Greenland's coast appeared two days later – a jagged line of white peaks rising from the grey sea.

"There!" croaked Leif, pointing to the distant curls of smoke above the Viking settlement. His voice was weak, but his spirit had returned.

The crew erupted in cheers. A surge of strength passed through every rower. Even the rescued fishermen found energy in their arms, and the battered longship cut across the water.

As they neared the harbour, the sounds of seabirds and crashing waves gave way to the roar of a waiting crowd. Erik the Red stood at the front, his red beard rippling in the wind. Behind him, families gathered, their eyes scanning the ship for loved ones – hope and worry etched on every face.

Sven searched the crowd, his heart racing. But he saw no sign of his family and felt a flicker of doubt. *Had they forgotten him?*

Leif stepped off the ship first. Though unsteady, he held himself straight and proud.

Erik grasped his son's shoulders. "Welcome home. Did you find what you were seeking?"

Leif's face broke into a grin. "We crossed the great sea. Sailed to the edge of the world. We found Vinland – its forests, wild game and warm winds. We bring back a shipful of riches … and stories worthy of the gods."

Erik chuckled. "Then tell me everything by the fire tonight." His smile faltered. "And Gamli?"

Leif's grin faded. He shook his head. "No."

Erik bowed his head. "He'll be missed. But I see you brought a shipwrecked crew home – that's lucky."

"Ha!" Leif laughed. "That's what Gamli always said."

"Did he now?" Erik turned to the crowd. "Let all Greenland hear! From this day forth, my son is no longer Leif Erikson – he is *Leif the Lucky Erikson!*"

A roar of approval thundered around the harbour.

Sven smiled. The name couldn't have been more fitting.

As the noise died down, Leif beckoned Thora forward. "When I was swept into the sea, this one took command. She faced down Thor's own fury and brought us through the storm. She's a true descendant of Aud the Deep-Minded – bold and brave." He turned to his father. "She deserves a ship of her own."

Erik nodded. "Then it shall be so. Thora the Brave shall command her own vessel."

Cheers rose again. Thora beamed, and her eyes met Sven's. In that look, he knew she'd accomplished what she'd set out to do – Thora had proved herself worthy.

"Well earned, Thora the Brave," said Sven.

Then Leif clapped Sven on the back. "And what of you, Sven? What name should the skalds sing for you?"

Sven shrugged. "I don't think any poet will remember me."

"Sven, you steered us through sea and storm, and saved my life," reminded Leif. "Gamli the Great lives on in you. You deserve a name."

Thora winked at Sven. "Rat or Goat Boy don't seem quite heroic enough, do they?" she teased. "And you're no longer a wolf pup – "

"Hey!" barked a familiar husky voice. "I was wrong about you."

Sven tensed. He turned to Bryn, who was standing with her arms crossed, but smiling.

"You weren't a bad omen," she said. "You were our good luck talisman."

She pulled her silver Thor's hammer from beneath her tunic and placed it around his neck. "For strength," she said. "And for storms still to come."

Sven was too stunned to speak. But no words were needed.

"*Sven?*"

He spun to see his mother emerging from the crowd. Close behind was his father.

"I didn't recognise you," said his mother, her eyes brimming with tears. She cupped his weathered face in her hands and kissed his forehead.

"By Thor's beard … what have you become?" said his father, eyeing the toughened lad before him.

"I can answer that, Askel," said Leif. "Your son is a sailor, a warrior and an explorer. He's a true Viking."

Sven's father grinned. And for the first time in his life, Sven felt his father's pride in him.

A sudden voice called out, "Eh, *wolf pup*! We thought you'd drowned!"

Sven looked over to see his older brothers, Bjorn and Torsten, elbowing their way forwards.

"You still jumping at shadows, *wolf pup*?" said Torsten, smirking.

The old name stung, but this time Sven didn't shrink away.

"Don't call him that, you sheep-brained oafs!" Thora snapped, throwing an arm around him. "Sven is a wolf of the sea."

Bjorn and Torsten blinked in disbelief, as the fierce shield-maiden defended their younger brother.

Leif barked a laugh. "That's it! Let it be known that Sven, son of Askel, is henceforth called Sea Wolf!"

There was another cheer from the crowd. A dozen hands clapped Sven on the back, nearly knocking him off his feet.

His father drew him into a bear hug. "Come. Let's get a fire going. I want to hear everything about your voyage."

As his family began the walk home, Sven lingered at the longship, fingers trailing across

its splintered hull. He gazed out at the grey sea, breathing in the salt air. He thought of Gamli, and everything the old sailor had taught him – wind, waves, stars and strength. He thought of Teyo, and the carved talisman buried in Vinland's soil. Of Thora, once a rival, now a friend. And of the storms and monsters they'd faced together.

But most of all, he thought of how far he'd come. How Leif the Lucky had shown him that courage is to row on despite the fear.

As a result, he had journeyed to the edge of the world.

And returned a Sea Wolf.

Glossary

Draugr	the dead, risen from their graves
gunwale	the upper edge of a boat's or ship's side
Helluland	thought to be Baffin Island, Canada
húðfat	sleeping bag
Jörmungandr	large sea serpent of Norse mythology
listed	(sailing term) tilted to one side
Markland	thought to be Labrador, Canada
Muspelheim	realm of fire in Norse mythology
rune	letters of the alphabet carved into stone or wood
Tafl	strategy board game similar to chess
Thor	the Norse god of thunder, son of Odin
turnshoes	a type of leather shoe
Valhalla	great hall of Odin, where worthy warriors live after dying in battle
Vinland	thought to be Newfoundland, Canada
whetstone	any stone used for sharpening a blade

Book talk questions

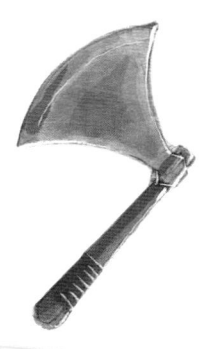

How does Sven change throughout the book from a wolf pup to Sea Wolf?

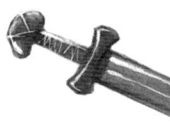

How are Gamli and Leif important to Sven in the book?

What adventures do you think Sven will face next?

Did you identify with any character in the story?

Which skills and values must a true Viking have?

Would you have done anything differently to any of the characters?

Do you know any Viking myths?

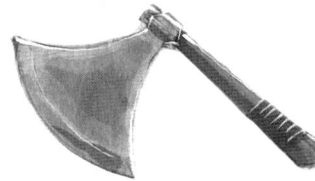

Which part of the book was the most exciting to read?

Did you learn anything from this book about Vikings?

How does Thora's family legacy impact her throughout the book?

Ask the author

Who is your favourite character in the book?
Gamli for his wisdom and humour. He is the first in the crew to take Sven under his wing and help him become a true Viking.

Chris Bradford

What are your favourite Viking stories?
I like the story of *Jörmungandr*, the Midgard Serpent in Norse myth. Cast into the sea by the war god Odin, it grew so huge it encircled the world. Then, in Ragnarok, the serpent rises to poison the sky and battle Thor, the god of thunder.

What's the best thing about being an author?
Inspiring young people to read! A good story can change a person's life and make them see the world in a different way – just like a voyage to the edge of the world!

Which character would you choose to take on a Viking voyage?
I'd choose Thora. She's courageous, fierce and clever. Just the sort of person you need on a dangerous voyage.

What was the biggest challenge you faced when writing *Sea Wolf*?
Learning about Norse myths and the Viking gods and fitting this knowledge naturally into the story.

Is there any topic you haven't written about yet that you would like to explore?
After writing about Samurai and Vikings, I'd love to explore the Aztecs and their culture.

When you're not writing, what do you like to do?
I love travelling. I recently visited Iceland and Sweden, one of the Viking homelands. In Reykjavik, the capital of Iceland, there is a statue of Leif Erikson. This inspired me to write about the great explorer and his voyage to Vinland.

Are there any particular authors or books that influenced your writing style?
For this story, I was influenced by the Viking Sagas. I wanted to create a story of bold adventures, great deeds and Viking gods so that the book wasn't just an exciting read, but the reader learnt about the Viking culture too.

Published by Collins
An imprint of HarperCollins*Publishers*

The News Building
1 London Bridge Street
London SE1 9GF
UK

Macken House
39/40 Mayor Street Upper
Dublin 1
D01 C9W8
Ireland

© HarperCollins*Publishers* Limited 2026

10 9 8 7 6 5 4 3 2 1

ISBN 978-0-00-878474-4

All rights reserved. No part of this publication may be reproduced, stored in a retrieval system, or transmitted in any form by any means, electronic, mechanical, photocopying, recording or otherwise, without the prior written permission of the Publisher or a licence permitting restricted copying in the United Kingdom issued by the Copyright Licensing Agency Ltd, 5th Floor, Shackleton House, 4 Battle Bridge Lane, London SE1 2HX.

Without limiting the exclusive rights of any author, contributor or the publisher of this publication, any unauthorised use of this publication to train generative artificial intelligence (AI) technologies is expressly prohibited. HarperCollins also exercise their rights under Article 4(3) of the Digital Single Market Directive 2019/790 and expressly reserve this publication from the text and data mining exception.

British Library Cataloguing-in-Publication Data
A catalogue record for this publication is available from the British Library.

Author: Chris Bradford
Illustrator: Eugenia Nobati (Advocate Art)
Publisher: Laura White
Commissioning editor: Holly Woolnough
Development editor: Zoë Clarke
Product manager: Holly Woolnough
Content editor: Selin Akca
Copyeditor: Sally Byford

Proofreader: Catherine Dakin
Reviewer: Lisa Davis
Fact checker: Sasha Morton
Cover designer: Sarah Finan
Internal designer: 2Hoots Publishing Services Ltd
Typesetter: David Jimenez
Production controller: Sophie Waeland

Collins would like to thank the teachers and children at Grange Primary School, Southwark, for being part of the development of Big Cat Read On.

Printed in the UK

MIX
Paper | Supporting responsible forestry
FSC® C006032

Made with responsibly sourced paper and vegetable ink

Scan to see how we are reducing our environmental impact.

Get the latest Collins Big Cat news at
collins.co.uk/collinsbigcat

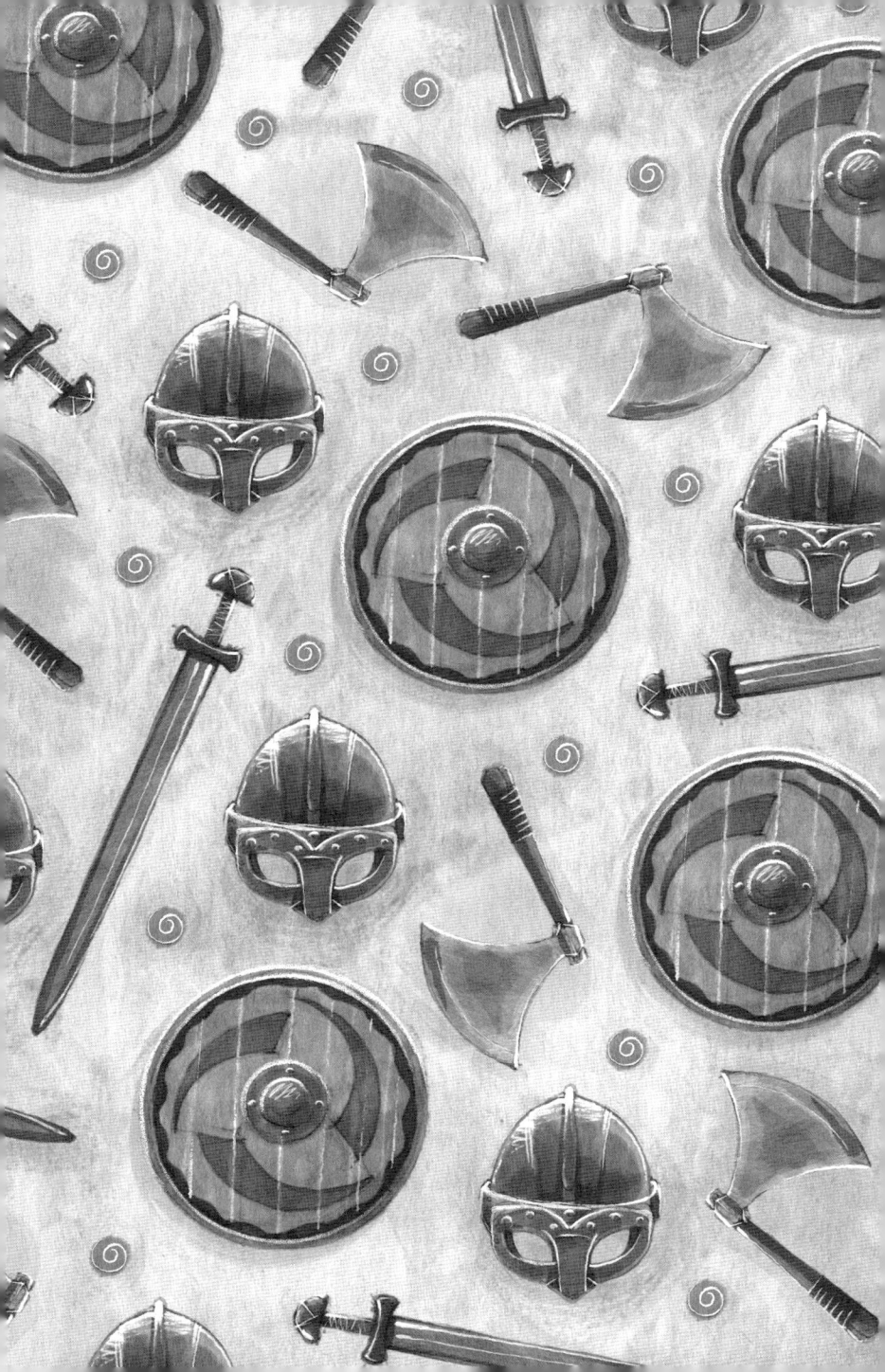